Connecting Entrepreneurs, Philanthropists and Influencers.

BUSINESS

BOOSTER TODAY MAGAZINE

THE #1 GERMANY BASED MAGAZINE FOR THE GLOBAL ENTREPRENEUR

I0390775

ÉRIC BEHANZIN
THE EXCLUSIVE
INTERVIEW

10X
YOUR GOALS

FIND YOUR
DEAL

BUSINESS
STRATEGY

**THE
EXPLOSIVE
BUSINESS
METHOD**

NO. 3|
JUNE 2019

CONTENT

COLUMNS AND DEPARTMENTS

FOUNDERS CORNER

By Sue Baumgärtner-Bartsch & Christian Bartsch

The first quarter of 2019, we have been focusing on expanding the magazine to new heights.

The Business Booster Today team has been diligently working on this goal. Having a vison and taking massive action leads to results. We can proudly say that **our magazine has now wings**.

Our magazine is now available through the e-Journal system in various **airlines**, such as Lufthansa, Swiss and Austrian to bring amazing value-added content from entrepreneurs and leaders in business to the world. We hear the saying often that the sky is the limit. For us the **sky is only the beginning**.

Being in the airlines brings our **reach to over 147 million passengers** and people who can enjoy the Business Booster Today content about business, growth and entrepreneurship while they fly to their next destination.

The entrepreneurial life is a **life of change** and can be challenging. But it also brings along opportunities for those who are ready to recognize them. The **5 traits of a successful entrepreneurs** are:

1. Focus on opportunities

2. Readily take action

3. Are highly motivated

4. Embrace change

5. Are on a mission

The reality of the entrepreneurial life is that risks will always be there to **create uncertainty**. Whether we talk about Brexit, challenges in the financial and economic markets or the climate changes and its effect on us as people. It does not matter. Every complaint there is, every problem that arises, every new product or service that gets launched comes with a degree of uncertainty and challenge.

Success means **overcoming this challenge**. The bigger the problem, the bigger the challenge, but also the bigger the **opportunity to add value and create success**. Taking action is not a gift but a habit, and in order to launch your products or services successfully, you have to commit to take he amounts of action in order to get attention. It is important to take action instead of planning to take action without ever getting anything done. Action is necessary to create success and can be the single defining quality. Average action gives you average results, while **massive action gives you extraordinary results**.

How can you be motivated in an environment that is keeping you at your status quo you may ask? That is exactly the point. In order to reach for the stars and **create extraordinary solutions** to people's problems, you have to put yourself in a state of mind to challenge your assumptions, beliefs and attitude.

Only when you are enthusiastic and believe in what you do makes an impact will you have the passion to keep going, even if things get tough along the way. Keep yourself focused on the goal and surround yourself with those **people who lift you and propel you to think** big like yourself to create that **breakthrough**. To succeed you need to be stimulated, excited, driven to some new action. Action that is goal-focused and mission driven. **Motivation is an inside job.** You need to create that fire in your belly and understand the underlying reason of why you are doing what you are doing. This will keep you highly motivated.

Entrepreneurs, innovators, thought leaders have all one thing in coming: They **embrace the change**, and keep an eye on what is coming next. Change is something that keeps successful entrepreneurs and leaders excited and is not something to be resisted. Apple and Steve Jobs are examples of this. He changes a product before a competitor can catch up or a consumer can get bored with them.

Business Boosters are **change makers** and are **entrepreneurs on a mission**. As entrepreneurs, we consider what we do not just a job but something that could forever change the world. If you do not think that way, you don't have a mission and you are not on a mission.

With the edition of the Business Booster Today Magazine, we are showcasing successful entrepreneurs and are providing a platform to share knowledge, to build bridges and to feature the **movers and shakers of the business world**. ✐

EDITORIAL TEAM

THE MOVERS AND SHAKERS
THE DREAM TEAM

Christian Bartsch

Publisher & Editor in Chief

Sue Baumgärtner-Bartsch

VP & Interview Editor

John Stokoe

Property Editor

Douglas Vermeeren

Leadership Editor

Orsi Beata Nagy

Business Processes Editor

Silvija Popovic

Mindset Editor

Udo Bartsch

Business Editor

Jan Erik Horgen

Investment Editor

Melody Garcia

Philanthropy Editor

Greg JC Granier

Entertainment Industry Editor

Michael Knulst

Business Editor

Eren Ünlü

Technology Editor

Aldrin-David Verburgt

VIP Stylist

Louis Kotze

Language Editor

Dalibor Kojic

Photographer

Marina Kotze

Health Editor

IMPRESS

ISSN (Print Edition)

2627-9223

ISSN (Online Edition)

2627-9231

ISBN-13

978-1-091459410

PUBLICATION DATE

27.03.2019

PUBLICATION SERIES INFO

March 2019 No. 3

PUBLICATION REVISION ID

2019-06-25-1

PUBLISHER & EDITOR IN CHIEF

Christian Bartsch

LEAD EDITOR & VP

Sue Baumgaertner-Bartsch

CONTRIBUTING EDITORS

Udo Bartsch, Douglas Vermeeren, Jan Erik Horgen, Michael Knulst, Louis Kotze, Orsi Beata Nagy, Sylvija Popovic, John Stokoe, Eren Ünlü, Greg JC Granier

CONTRIBUTING WRITERS

Michelle Davis, Robb Evans, Billy Gajic, Raluca Gomeaja, Marina Kotze, Sam Komeha, Kati Israel, Jaine Lopez, Vikas Malkani, Robert Martin, Milos & Danijela Nakovski, Christine Nielsen, Nina Peutherer, Richard Peutherer, Gavin Sim, Nina Schmid, Kirstie Shapiro, Tomer Sapir Spitkowski, Cristina Stavinski, Mona Tenjo, Janine Van Throo, Yasemin Yazan, Brett Yeager, Erwin Wils , Sabine Zettl

PHOTOGRAPHY, VIP STYLING & MAKEUP

Dalibor Kojic, Aldrin-David Verburgt

PUBLISHED BY

ACATO GmbH, 1st. Floor, Theresienhoehe 28, 80339 Munich, Germany

ADVERTISING & SALES

sales@businessboostertoday.com

Phone +49 89 54041070

www.businessboostertoday.com

SUBSCRIPTIONS

Booster club members: annual membership dues include €197 for a regular one-year subscription and €47 for an electronic member subscription. Non-members subscription rate are €97 for an electronic subscription. Change of address notices and subscriptions should be directed to BBT magazine.

THE EXPLOSIVE BUSINESS METHOD DRIVES INTERNATIONAL SUCCESS

Eric Behanzin

By Christian Bartsch (Germany)

As a child Eric was shy. Today he is a different person. Let me introduce to you who Eric is and what he has created with the power of his mind.

Who is Eric?

Having suffered a rather painful childhood, Eric Behanzin was shy. He has a passion for music and went on to enjoy a 20-year international career as a singer, musician and teacher. With over twelve years of entrepreneurial experience, Éric, now is a business coach, has created the "Explosive Business" method, and gives his corporate customers the keys to multiplying their financial results in just a few months.

Where is his business now?

Explosive Business is an international organization that coaches entrepreneurs to scale up their business by adding millions of dollars in sales revenue in a few months.

They have Private Clubs in multiple cities in Europe and have the ambition to open more Clubs across Europe, North America, Asia and Africa before the end of 2019.

What is he doing for them?

Their Private Clubs clients are hand picked high-level entrepreneurs that already master their businesses and are looking at increasing, even more, their reach and impact with their products and services.

They lead their clients to position themselves as a premium solution in their industry, so that they can maximize their profits

fast and add even more value to their offers.

This is not wishful thinking, Explosive Business went from 0 to 5.2 millions of dollars in 18 months and served several clients to explode their business. From 70k to 3M in a year, 150k to 1.3M in 8 months, 0 to 195k in 6 months and so on.

How does he do it?

People will seriously ask how Eric gets his clients to go beyond their business limits. People often believe there is a ceiling to their business where they can not go beyond.

We block our own potential?

This barrier only exists in the human mind. It is given to us all by society, education, and historical failures in life.

When we **overcome this barrier** in our mind, the world turns from a flat disk into a fast moving ball. Then we are able to play the ball as we desire. Of course there are other players on the field that also want this ball. This is **no reason** for us to hold back. It motivates us to continue as this is a game. It is the true game of life.

We do not want to sit on the side watching and complaining about our life. Is your life as an entrepreneur or desiring startup limited?

Eric will **blast out** that dust covering your success in life, business and legacy. Life should not just be about filling the day with a *boring and unhappy* activity.

The joy you can experience when you **close a high ticket client** provides you with Adrenalin that is indescribable. It **will propel your passion** to take your business forward. Your body feels a rush of blood, joy and motivation.

This transforms your attitude. Good attitude is nice. Great attitude is contagious.

Why is Eric's coaching so different?

As you can see in many of Eric Behanzin's coaching videos people are **experiencing something very different** in their lives. It is not an experience

that lasts for a few days. They turn their lives around. They get rid of stuff that keeps them off their goals. May it be unfitness, weight, smoking, late night drinking or even other bad habits.

If you want to explode your business, you have to do what ever it takes. Really? Well, for Eric it has to be in a **healthy balance**. The unhealthy life he left behind.

In a recent conversation with Eric I got an insight in some of his **life concepts**.

What a deep conversation with Eric can provide?

After having meet Eric twice, one afternoon we used the time to discuss his life experience of having gone on a life changing diet. Well, that was not really a diet. It was much more. He did not eat or drink anything. His mind kept telling him, he would starve to death. His mind kept telling him if he would continue 3 more days fasting, he would die.

It was his mind. It was so used to having the **abundance of food**

we all believe to be healthy. In fact, he did not die. After 12 days of going through this **unique experience** he came out a different person. The emotions, the thoughts and the realization of **what life is**, helped him write an impactful book.

With his book „12 days", he created an inspiring story of an entrepreneur who went 12 days alone without food or water, creating a method to make you rich, happy and proud of

yourself. Eric states that in his book that the most effective way to become rich is to be an entrepreneur. Everything is possible once you have a clearly defined vision.

The keys he is giving in this book will help entrepreneurs make at least 1 million Euros per years. Eric believes further that there is a massive difference between a millionaire and a billionaire:

> "Millionaires change their own lives, but billionaires change the lives of millions more."- Eric Behanzin

The change in self valuation?

The greatest impacts to his life were the fasting and advice he received. It changed his valuation of his service, talents and results.

He changed his belief in what his coaching was worth. Even for corporate clients his new approach made him drive his business to an unforeseen level.

Which insights a 2nd encounter can provide?

As we continued later in the evening our conversation in a bar in Paris, I noticed that we both had similar habits to propell the efficiency of our personal activities.

The influence of smartphones on our concentration and health is often ignored by consumers. Some employers have woken up but have difficulties to handle generations that are used to communicating via their devices instead of **having a meaningful conversation**.

Smartphones are reducing our

level of concentration as they keep buzzing, vibrating or making all sorts of distracting actions. People keep looking towards their phone or stop their work and play for ages with their phone until realizing they have lost valuable work time.

In a family situation this can even lead to relationship breaking up as this becomes a difficult to control habit. I usually leave my phone on silence away from sight when I am working. Eric has gone a much more drastic step. **He got rid of the phone and has seen his level of concentration going up extremely.**

He says that balance does not exist, only priorities. And so even if his biggest multi-million-dollar client may be clamoring for a promise he has not delivered, he remains unreachable. **He truly believes that your marriage and your family are more important than your career. Boom!**

How to increase the game level in life and business?

Other entrepreneurs want to gain such levels of success, too. He shows them what to do.

As the discussion with health risks of the 5G networks procceeds, Eric is way ahead of time. That is why he can concentrate on his transformational activities.

Transformational vs transactional activities

Nevertheless, he had to realize at a point in his entrepreneurial career that he had to let go of transactional activities. He could not achieve such a vital change in his activities without building a powerful team to rely on.

He handed over the transactional tasks to his CEO Sabrina. This explosive business has its team of highly motivated and powerful coaches and trainers.

What are the keys to exploding revenues?

Eric is very much aware what makes businesses grow and survive beyond the storms of economies. His clients gather confidence in their own products. They are enabled to position their products as a unique premium product in their market niches.

This drives their revenue from a 5 figure to a 6 figure just in months. **They had to change their way of thinking. That changed their way of selling.**

People love buying, but they do not like being sold to. Selling is persuading your client that the best way for them to change their life and business is for them to buy your product. But the client must never be forced. In the book "12 days", Eric speaks about creating a "Star Offer". It fulfills three conditions:

- It is irresistible to your clients.
- It is ultra-profitable for you.
- It is easier for you to deliver.

Systematisation and Consistency

In order to make this a sustainable way of doing business, Eric has made it easier for his clients to develop consistent results. He went to systemize the process using his explosive business method.

The "Explosive Business" method in short:

1. Maximize Profits

2. Scale Without You

3. Build to Sell

The explosive business method is for speakers, entrepreneurs, coaches, investors, authors and consultants. Eric says there are three fundamental pillars that a business leader must implement to increase the company's revenue, namely:

a.   Clarity: A clear vision and culture that everyone understands.

b.   Focus: to concentrate only on actions that can have a massive impact and

c.   Courage: to be ready to transform the company radically if necessary.

A lot of people and businesses focus on the how and what that they get lost and life passes. Eric challenges everyone to ask yourself these powerful questions:

"What is your message?"

"What do you want to say to the world?"

"What do you want to leave as a legacy?"

Growth is never linear but exponential. With Eric's business method, growth is explosive!

We do not grow and help others to grow by chance but by change.

For more information about Eric go to:

www.explosivebusiness.com

BUILDING AND GROWING BUSINESSES WITH THE RIGHT PEOPLE

By Sue Baumgaertner-Bartsch (Germany)

Some burn contacts in step 1

Life and business are about the people we meet. Nowadays, we have social media, we have Facebook and all these great tools, but what I do not like at all is when people contact me and the first thing, they do is try to sell me something. I am sure you have had this experience too. Or how about when people send you a message and ask what you do via LinkedIn, instead of looking at your profile first **to better understand** what you are doing and to ask an interesting question to start building a relationship?

Build relationships first

We live in a fast-paced world, where people sometimes do not take the time to get to know others at first.

If you want to be successful in business, you need to understand that it takes **9-12 touch points** with **potential customers** before they get to know and trust you and buy from you. That is why your personal branding is so important. Do you know what people say about you when you are not in the room? This is how they see you.

Get to know the person

Show a sincere interest in the other person and get to know them, and **build a relationship**. Think also what you can do for others first. Especially if you meet people who are more successful than you are, refrain from talking about yourself and giving advice.

Successful people could care less about your opinion. Rather ask them questions and get to know the other side. Get to **know their interests and hobbies**. If you have an opportunity to research them before you meet them, then do so. This will help you start an interesting conversation and will set you apart from the normal and average business people who do not have a clue about the other person and come across as uninformed.

Getting most out of business events

Whenever you go to business events and meetings, find out from the website and the event organizer about the invited guests, or key note speakers. This will help you **be ahead of the game** from all the others who do not take the time to prepare for an event.

No matter what you do: Whether you have an upcoming business meeting, get to meet an influential person, speak in front of an audience or coach people, you want to prepare yourself.

Preparation is key in everything I do, and I have noted the difference of simply just "showing up" versus **preparing myself ahead** of time. The results are different. You will shine brighter, have deeper conversations and make a greater impact in the lives and businesses of others.

Anticipate what will come

When you prepare, ask yourself what it is that you can bring to the table. Anticipate how your meeting could go and be yourself. You **do not have to know everything**, and it is ok to admit when you do not know something, because that shows you are not a "know-it-all" person, but rather someone who is sincere and authentic.

Ask lots of questions, especially have the other person talk 80% of the time and you only 20% of the time, if the other person is more successful than you are.

Once you have met somebody at an event for example, it does not stop there. You want to build that relationship. And that means, you want to **follow up with that person**.

Successful relationships are all about the follow up and follow throughs! How many people have you met that tell you they will give you a call back and never actually do?

Do not say something and do the opposite thing!

Partners need to be more than just talkers

I highly value sincerity, honesty, integrity and reliability in working with my business partners. I also partner up with A-players. It is important that you understand people and **what drives them**, so that you find the right people to work with you.

If you pay attention to the people around you and the people you meet, you will find that it often takes that **one person to meet and build a relationship with** or that one meeting you go to when new opportunities come your way.

"Business as I say is about the people you meet and the relationships you build. Pay attention to the people you meet and those you want to meet, and always act from a place of authenticity."- Sue Baumgaertner-Bartsch

Exercise: Make a list of the top 10 people that you want to meet and get to know who you think would be of value to you and your business growth.

It takes on average 4- 5 connections to meet and **get to know that person**. If you think big, you will reach big. If you think it is possible, it will be possible.

Once you have made that list, find out as much as you can about them. Find out, for example, what they read, what the like to do in their free time as a hobby, where these **people socialize and network**, where you can meet them or how to otherwise connect with them. This could be business events, this could be through a social activity or another connection you have.

It takes an **effort and real curiosity** on your part, and time. But imagine you meet that one person that you wanted to meet and then you have your opportunity-that is when you want to show up prepared, ready and able to build that relationship. Go for it! ✒

GAIN YOUR SUCCESS

MASTERMIND TOPICS

Defining Your Product

Types of Product Benefits

Identifying Your Market

Developing Product Campaigns

Ensuring the Success of Campaigns

Segmenting Your Market

Launching a Product

Post-Product Launch Mandatories

Promoting Your Product

Facts and Figures

MASTERING THE ART OF SELLING PRESENTATION

WWW.GAINYOURSUCCESS.COM

5 QUESTIONS TO CHECK THE SUCCESS OF YOUR BUSINESS

By Raluca Gomeaja (France)

Success! People may look at success from different angles depending on education, experience, values and much more. When coming to business success there are a few things that may indicate how profitable, value added and sustainable your business really is!

Many strategies have been defined in order to increase business profit, to reduce cost, to take better care of employees!

Yet a shift is happening in the way the world is going, growing and progressing; as its changing at the level of people making business themselves; most of the new graduates which are generally called millenniums are no longer looking at the traditional way of doing business and not very much attracted by traditional corporations; it is no longer only about figures; is how sustainable those figures are and what can define success!

In this **new innovative way of doing business** here are my personal beliefs linked to 5 essential questions to ask in order to make a difference:

1. How successful is your team?

No matter if you are a mid-manager in a corporation or a small size/big size business owner your team will define your success! A successful entrepreneur wants to attract the best!

The question is why the best shall come and work for them? When your team is successful not only you see it in results and the work environment but they are "radiating"/shining outside the business.

Make sure your people are successful; they are your most important capital! You may consider understanding what they think success is, you may consider sharing profit

with them, have a team coach to help them grow as a successful team etc. And there are ways to measure it as well!

2. How successful are your clients?

This is probably the oldest definition of success in business: **you don't exist if your clients are not buying what you propose**; why they buy from you: mostly because they need/want what you propose and they are happy with you.

Yet if you work with someone that has no capability of continue buying whatever you are selling, well there will no longer be a business, especially if you depend on that client entirely! Make sure you work with successful clients:

how many clients do you have, what are their results, what are their plans for the future, etc?

3. How successful are your stakeholders?

How happy is the community around you with what you do? How much additional values does your business bring to them?

Most of the time businesses focus so much on figures that they forgot what may create their success or their fail: people around them.

Have a look at the community, what is their interest, how can you add something to their life, why shall they be happy to have you as part of their environment?

4. How successful is your footprint, the environmental impact?

We talk a lot about environment these days and yet not enough in relation with business success!

Some businesses consider they have no direct

impact on it, so it's not their core preoccupation; some others believe that they do enough to balance some of their negative impact; but let's be honest:

how sustainable can you be if what you do is not respectful to the world you operate in; and this goes way beyond general environment measures; this come within the DNA of the business owner: lead by example, show a different way of doing business with 0 compromise on this one! There is no other way for any successful business to be.

5. How successful is your model?

This more than anything will define your current and future success! What is that you do that makes a difference? How relevant is what you do and for whom?

What is it that your business is bringing to the world? What is your value added? New businesses are created every day, old businesses are still there to provide in a traditional way; look further, think of what it is that you can add to this world and **before thinking about success, think about your impact first!**

"If I were to just try to follow or pretend I was somebody else, it wouldn't be the most true and distinctive version of my highest leadership." Abby Falik

LEADERSHIP BEFORE MANAGEMENT

By Douglas Vermeeren (Canada)

Personal Power Mastery Moment

Progress is something that many average people think just happens for others. Their pattens are concerned more with **staying comfortable and secure**. These individuals don't often see value in stretching to create more. (Even though they are the ones who benefit most.)

The reason why is that they are generally content with the **patterns in their lives** as they currently exist and they have settled in. As I have observed people who have attended my seminars and compared them to the **top achievers I interviewed** I think there is one thing that gets people started on the path of progress and that thing is to simply begin asking more questions.

The persuit of answers

Questions in our lives are the primer that begins our pursuit of answers. And the better the questions are that we ask the higher our levels of answers become. As we **ask deep searching questions** about our **behaviours and situations** we can begin to recognize that we are capable of levelling everything up.

It has often been said that if you want to level up your life, level up the kinds of questions you ask about it.

Avoid answers leading to temporary results

Too often the question that people get hung up on is What can they do?

Specifically they are talking about **tactics, strategies and check-lists**. These kinds of things often create quick but temporary results. Tactics can't often be maintained because they focus on activity.

These are what I call **management activities**. You are essentially managing your daily activities and they are **constantly shifting and changing** depending on what is occurring in your life.

Best approach to questions

I am going to recommend you start with another kind of questions first. To make your management questions **more effective start** asking leadership questions. Leadership questions don't reflect as much on what to do as why to do.

Leadership questions focus on purpose and power. What is the real direction you want your life to take? Why do you want these things in your life? How does this **contribute to the legacy** you wish to create and what will the ultimate rewards and circumstance look like? Are these the things you really want?

Establishing leadership

As you establish leadership before management you will find that your management begins to have purpose.

This is the result of questions.

My interviews of top achievers

When I first started my interviews with eh worlds top achievers I learned about the power of questions through one of the interviews I conducted. This gentleman who most would never know was a successful business man and also **very balanced with family and home life**.

As I asked him how he did it he pulled out a notebook and showed me that he had a list of around 100 questions he read and considered every Sunday afternoon.

The reflections of an interview

He confessed that as he grew so did the nature of his questions. His questions seemed to reflect several **different areas of his life** (if you look closely they are very similar to the 5 pillars we teach in Personal Power Mastery.)

In reflection each week he would consider how his life measured up to some of the questions in his list. As a result he would often come away with **new goals for the week**, a renewed way of looking at things and some feelings of progress based on what had happened the previous week.

What I learned

This strategy was so impressive to me that I began to do the same and have also taught it to many of our students in Personal Power Mastery since. While I am not going to request that you make a list of 100 questions to review weekly (You can if you wish and it would help you a lot)

I am going to give as **your challenge today** to simply take a moment and come up with 10 questions you can ask yourself about what you want and how things are going in your life. Make them searching questions to explore where you are at in your life today and how you could improve your situation.

Remember you must lead your life before you can manage it. ✐

BUSINESS STRATEGY

"We have entered a new era: many of the old business models with their related revenue models don't seem to work anymore. There is a whole new dynamic and as entrepreneur we have to shift our old paradigms and ways of thinking."

By Michael Knulst (The Netherlands)

Why are you in Business? What is the value of your Business? Are you in the right Business?

Many consultants emphasize that business strategy is necessary and I agree with that. The main question however is how to do this? In most articles and blog posts I read, the authors only keep on mentioning that strategy is very important and that's it. Being an entrepreneur myself I am much more interested in the next step; How to do this?

Strategic thinking

Most business owners, who struggle, are busy with the day to day of their business and take action on what's appealing. They started with some sort of idea on a product or service **based on emotional reasons**. Instead of developing a solid business plan, they just start enthusiastically without thoroughly thinking their business through. And that's the tricky art. After all, if you fail to plan, you plan to fail.

Another category is often struggling not only with developing a business plan but developing an **overall strategy** for conducting business. It's not always that people don't know how to develop a plan. Often times small business entrepreneurs do know how to **develop their strategy**, but they simply don't. They think skipping the planning will get them to market sooner.

It often times seems so much easier to conduct small business practices, that a plan would be overkill. However, in a small business, a small mistake can have a **greater impact** for a longer duration if it's in regard to a core business model broken or objective lost.

The third category has too much of a focus on earnings instead of value. They lack long term vision and they are actually digging their own grave. So, in the situations mentioned above we find the main reasons why so many small businesses struggle is their lack of a strategic plan. Strategic entrepreneurs finally, know their vision, develop different alternatives for its accomplishment, choose the approach they think is most probable and intensively monitor their progression.

Strategic planning

In the past I have been working quite a lot with the Strategic Business planning process. This usually started with a one- or two-day brainstorm sessions, somewhere in a nice resort. One of the participants worked everything out and it all ended up in a plan of 25 pages or more. The only problem was that after this plan was presented, in most cases, everybody started running and nobody ever looked back into the wonderfully produced strategic document any more.

I eventually found out that Strategic Business Planning does not work for an unknown future, where speed seems to dictate our choices. It occurred to me that in many cases the success of a business is determined by the **quality of its Business model**. A Business model describes the rationale of how an organization creates, delivers and captures value. In other words; Your Business model represents the strategic blueprint of your organization.

I found it remarkable that many entrepreneurs do not exactly know what their business model is. For the past 6 years I have been consistently working with developing business models and the first step is to evaluate your current one. Personally, I like the **Business model canvas** from **Alex Osterwalder**. This is a strategic management and entrepreneurial tool that allows you to describe, design, challenge, invent and pivot your business model.

Goal setting

Setting goals is an essential step in the strategic planning, no matter what method or canvas you are using. Writing your goals really down is the **driving force** in order to prevent you from the trap of mediocrity. Written goals provide you with clarity of outcome, which is a prerequisite for becoming an outstanding decision maker. Why is this so important? It all has to do with how our brains work. Our brains are incredibly complex. We can sift through billions of bits of data at any given time. And somehow, so we don't short circuit, we have to organize that information. The **Reticular Activating System** helps with that. The Reticular Activating System is a bundle of nerves at our brainstem that **filters out unnecessary information** so the important stuff gets through. You can train your Reticular Activating System by taking your subconscious thoughts and marrying them to your conscious thoughts. They call it "setting your intent." This basically means that if you focus hard on your goals, your Reticular Activating System will reveal the people, information and opportunities that help you achieve them.

Now it comes upon mastering your focus so that **achieving your goals** happens quickly and automatically. The primary benefit of mastering goal setting and focusing on their realization is that you are in control. The irony by contrast however is that most people spend more time planning their summer vacations than they do planning their business. Most people major in minor things. The majority of SME entrepreneurs invest their time, money and **energy in the wrong way**! They get caught up in the things that keep them busy but contribute very little to the overall quality of their business and lives.

Execution

Once you have your strategy (business model) and goals in place, more than ever, it is of vital importance that your plans are executed fast and without failure. Executing strategy -getting the right things done- has become the **new differentiator** in today's economy. In order to keep your focus on your goals and the relentless execution of them, I prefer to work with roadmaps. A strategic roadmap for example, is a visualization of your business strategy with a clear overview of what actions are needed to help your company achieve its long-term goals; on every level in your business. Your roadmap is the **blueprint** of your business; it connects the dots for people in your organization by showing everyone how their everyday actions fit with the company's vision of where it wants to be in the future. The right roadmap supports the alignment of strategy, execution and control, making organisations successful in implementing their strategic goals fast. ✒

HOW AUTOMOTIVE DEALERSHIPS CAN

Turn Good Deeds into Better Business

By Sam Komeha (USA)

Though the season of giving is officially behind us, it's still important to be charitable throughout the year. While it's nice for individuals to donate their time and money to worthy causes, for **automotive dealerships** these **charitable acts** can lead to more than just a feeling of goodwill.

There are many ways to give back to the community, but which types of charitable work are best for the community and for the dealership? The answer will depend heavily on what type of work the dealership is looking to do, what type of impact they would like it to have, both for their business and for the community. The following ideas for charitable work and donations are feasible for every automotive dealership and the **returns gained** from these acts of kindness will be **substantial.**

Volunteer as a Group

Getting your whole team together to work toward a common goal outside of the dealership is a great way to form stronger relationships, help the community, and advertise the dealership. Doing things like roadside litter clean up, working in soup kitchens and food pantries, or volunteering for large nonprofits, like Habitat for Humanity or Salvation Army, will make a huge local impact and help to get the dealership's name out there.

To further the **positive impact on the business**, volunteers can wear bold colored shirts with the **company's name and logo** on them. This is especially important when working in public areas, like in parks or along the roads for litter cleanup, because these shirts will serve as advertisements and increase the dealership's public image.

Some other volunteering ideas for groups include:

- Improving community parks
- Meals on   Wheels
- Visiting nursing homes

- Local humane   society
- Community garden

Hold Donation Drives

Throughout the year, in every community, there are people in need of donations. The list of things that can be donated is nearly endless. From food to clothing to blood, different nonprofits are always looking for businesses to team up with to serve as drop off locations and increase the number of donations they receive.

By **holding a donation drive** or agreeing to be a drop off location for a nonprofit's donations, **dealerships will attract more people** to their lot as they come to donate goods. They will also gain a more positive public image for taking part in important causes. During these drives, dealerships may want to have a special or incentive to help get more people to the lot to donate and to get the donors to look around a bit while they're there. By simply being hospitable to a local charity, dealerships will have a huge charitable impact without investing a lot of time or resources.

Other types of donation drives include:

- Mobile blood donation
- Non-perishable food
- Home Goods
- Toys
- Books

Become a Local Sponsor

There are always local organizations looking for sponsors. Recreational sports teams, academic teams, and other groups that usually rely on fundraising sales and parent contributions can benefit greatly from having a local sponsor. **As a sponsor**, the dealership won't be responsible for all the group's expenses, but they can help with certain aspects of the group's costs.

When sponsoring a local group, automotive dealerships should be sure to advertise their contributions. They may have their company name or logo on the team shirts, create a banner, or make note of their sponsorship on local advertisements. By making their contributions known, dealerships will be able to help local residents while increasing their business.

Some other groups that may need a local sponsor are:

- Travelling humanitarian groups
- Special Olympic teams
- Youth sports
- Academic teams
- Pageant contestants

Smart Dealerships are Charitable Dealerships

When automotive dealerships give back to their communities, they are creating an **opportunity to improve their public image** and **advertise their business**. Though the overall goal of donating and volunteering should be to help those in need, the bonus of creating more business for the dealership is a great incentive to get out and do some good in the world. ✒

WITHOUT BUSINESS SYSTEMS YOU ARE GOING TO FAIL!

By Orsi B. Nagy (United Kingdom)

Most new businesses fail within the first 18 months from starting for 2 reasons: they either run out of money or their business lack of systems. Often business owners who hear the word "systems" straight away think some kind of a software. Systems do not necessarily mean software of any sort. Software are tools that help us to run our businesses more efficiently. When we talk about systems, we refer to **business operating systems**. How we operate our business. It is a **standard, enterprise-wide collection of business processes** used in many diversified industrial companies.

Most start-ups, whether they are companies or entrepreneurs, don't realise the importance having business operation systems in place. They don't realise that they have to systemize their business in order for it to **run effectively**, on the right time scale, to increase their profit continuously and increase the value of the business in case they get to the point of selling it.

I often wonder why it is not a priority for them? The reason is that most business owners are the ones who think big, who have the visions and see the **big picture** and forget to pay attention to the basics. They also might lack the right team around them to take charge of these tasks. I don't think we live in a world where we can afford ignoring the basics.

As a business system expert I can clearly see when a business runs **on an ad hoc basis**. They are all over the place, there are no strategies, they lack of a plan and their focus is mostly on making money. If you don't invest time and energy in seeing and understanding how you operate your business from social media platforms, through your selling procedures to customer complains then soon you are going to be part of the failed businesses' **statistics**, and out of business. But do you want to be part of the statistics of the companies who manages to grow their profit year after year? I'm sure you do!

I used to work with a healthy food store where due to several reasons selling didn't go well in the shop. Soon the owner realised what the problem was: location! However, to move the shop to the right location in **London required long time and great amount of money** as the competition was very hot amongst the already established well known food and café chains. So, the owner decided to make the most out what they have till the current lease runs out.

The store also had a webshop and that was the key for the time being. Together, we checked what we were **selling on the webshop** and increased the variety of the products. This resulted in more online orders than ever before. We checked which are the most favourite items and regularly run reports on the favourite items so we ensured the stock had enough to fulfil the demand.

Increased sales brought another problem: increased customer complains. The team had no idea how to handle the problem and the only thing they could think of was issuing refunds with the simple reason: we are dealing with food. Needless to say, this **resulted in even more complaints** as the clients figured out that anything they complain about, they get a refund so they started to take advantage of this.

First, we examined what kind of complaints the company received and why they kept getting them. Once we saw the patterns of errors then we determined different complain categories. This allowed us to see the whole picture and we started putting together an **improvement strategy**. We created different processes for tackling the different issues. Started with a process for packaging of the orders. This mitigated the unnecessary damage to the items inside the box. We also created another **process for customer complaints**, how they should complain, in what form and set a time limit for the complaints.

This process directed all complaints to one place, the customers had to complain within 48 hours of receiving their package. We introduced an "thank you and info card" that thanked for the order but also informed the customers about the complaint process in case they are not happy with anything. We ensured that this card was **the first thing they saw** when they opened their order. This was a simple solution but it reduced the customer complaints by 93%!

Just imagine how much time, energy and stress we released for the staff with this simple process! This exercise didn't take long to do and implement. Also it allowed the team to have more focus on other things that improved the sales.

I believe on a regular basis we have to go back to basics. We have to examine:

- What processes we have in place if we have any at all?
- How do these processes run? Effectively or not?
- Does everybody understand them and their purpose?
- Do they still serve the purpose at all?
- Do they need improvement?
- Is there an opportunity to improve them?

However sometimes there are no direct signs of a problem and you have to dig deeper. There is an easy way to figure out if a task needs a process or the existing process desperately needs an update. Analyse them and see what tasks are **costing you the most** money or the most time or in some cases both!

The next thing you need to do is to see whether these tasks can be: automated, outsourced or save time on and scale them? Investigate, **find the problems**, find the solutions for them, create the process, teach the people who will use the process and update it when necessary.

The opportunities of improvements are endless and always bring us challenges. Don't let these challenges deter you from your path! You shouldn't be afraid of them. I guarantee you that when **you are able to handle these** you will see the results of them. ✐

BUSINESS INTRODUCTIONS

BIOVETA - BEAUTIFUL HAIR SHAMPOO PRODUCTS

Bioveta is a family of unique products which provide synergistic support in a very organic and sophisticated manner. We supply revolutionary products that work. Bioveta's advanced research ensures that we provide and maintain the absolute finest products available to date. From your hair to your toes, inside and out, Bioveta has a plan to create a whole new healthier you.

BioVeta, LLC, Dallas, Texas, USA

www.bioveta.com

AUTOMOTIVE SERVICE TAGS REDUCE COSTS & WASTE

We have insider knowledge of dealerships and their service departments, which gives us the opportunity to look at the wasteful, ineffective areas of the industry and develop products to make them more efficient. Currently, one of the most unnecessary costs of dealership service departments is the thousands of dollars' worth of paper auto service tags they throw away each year.

New Generation Service Tags, LLC, Chevy Chase, MD, USA

www.newgenerationservicetags.com

WE BOOST MEDIA CREDIBILITY AND VISIBILITY

Do you want to diversify your business into multiple countries? This seams an impossible task? It is all too complicated to get the international marketing for your brand going? We will boost your sales by 30% in 90 days with our strategies and platforms. Don't waste your energy and budget on experiments!

PR Media Reach, Munich, Germany

www.PRMediaReach.com

GENERATE INCOME WITH PROPERTY IN VESTMENT IN THE UK

Learn how to successfully master the property investment in business. Our trainers are successful real estate investors with expertise in the banking and sourcing business. Our workshops provide you the knowledge so that deals come to you and how to create for yourself a bullet proof investor package. Our clients are successful in sourcing, generating returns of investment and building a recurring amount of deals with their investors.

Source My Property LTD, Cardiff, United Kingdom

www.SourceMYProperty.com/academy

MUMS ARE SUCCESSFUL FAMILY AND BUSINESS LEADERS

We help mum's who work from home to create a balanced, abundant life filled with fun and laughter. We have everything you need in one place. Here at Mum Academy we nurture you to give you the power to nurture yourself. We do this through virtual business coaching, conferences, global retreats, online peer support, inspirational reading, online courses and training videos.

Mum Academy, Cardiff, United Kingdom

www.mumacademy.com

10X YOUR ACTIVITIES TO REACH YOUR GOALS

By Christian Bartsch (Germany)

Many people **want** to take their life in **a different direction**. They start a business. They try out all sorts of ideas. Sometimes they have **no ideas**. They just go for the apparently easy money. Then reality hits them. These are the companies that do not make it past their 1st birthday.

People often like to mix the words "business", "company" and "brands" up. Before I proceed here, lets remove the fog. A company is for me a legal entity. If I invent several different brands while using that single legal entity then it is still one company with a multitude of business ideas I am working on getting them into a sustainable energy level.

My business experience is based on work for some of top brands (incl. BMW, KPMG) and working on projects for a Microsoft Consultancy. Furthermore, I have learned a lot from my 3 companies (UK & Germany).

Experience success and failure

As you enter markets, start new products, test new marketing platforms and agree to joint ventures, you **experience success and failure** in close proximity to each other.

It is strange when a venture capital company sends me a birthday card for my company. Its been a year since my 3rd company had its 8th birthday. My first company was 10 years old before it was dissolved as the 3rd company had taken over most of its activities. So theoretically you could say its now 19 years old? Time to go to university.

During those many years I have met many interesting people. Some were very honourable and others very cheeky monkeys. When a client damages you by not paying a 6 figure bill then you know it is not easily forgotten. Nevertheless, you have to **move on** once you have exchanged a barrage of energy.

The value of a good guide

Had I had then **a good business coach**, I would have avoided a lot of pain, anxiety and loss of money. The next year I got my first business coach.

As your business grows you will eventually **outgrow your coach's expertise** if the coach is only focused on one particular expertise. The reality teaches us that we need a multitude of experts to provide us a complex solution we call business momentum.

Unfortunately, the education system does not really address the world of small to medium business. Students in schools and universities do not get the knowledge provided by **people you are actually in business**. Often if you are lucky they had some person working for them while they were working in a corporate job. This knowledge alone will not get your business to **become a speed boat**.

Whilst big corporations can out manoeuvre you with their massive cash flow and workforce, they are slow in turning corners. Therefore *Small Medium Entreprises* (SMEs) are capable of defeating a big giant although they have a small budget and only a handful of people wortking in a team.

What history teaches us

When you look at history, often smaller organisations and countries were able to defeat extreme powerful entities.

Look at what the teams at **Bletchley Park** (UK) did to break the encryption codes of the Enigma and other German coding systems during World War II. In order to succeed, the British assembled a team of mathematicians, Engineers, WRNS and civilian workers. The boring and unpleasant work conditions in the calculation machine rooms were endured by hundreds of female workers setting the parameters used to attempt to decode the enemy communication.

Multi talent teams succeed

When we take this example and transfer it to the agile world of smaller business operations, it becomes apparent that in order to succeed you need to assemble a multi talent team. By collection gonly people of one type of talent, you will fail. Therefore you need people that bring along different skills and knowledge but have one important common ground: their **commitment to the mission** everybody is working together to achieve.

The decoding operations run day and night to keep up with the speed the codes were being changed by the enemy.

Be a speed boat in the market

In a global economy **the speed of change** is even greater. So many new companies enter the market, add new ideas, solutions and concepts. The speed of implementation is unbelievable. The **threat to company secrets** are even greater with hacking and ransom ware attacks.

Therefore, you need to **increase your speed** of implementation, marketing and delivery by the factor of 10 to 100. If you continue on a **slow motion** you will be run over by smaller and larger competitors. The ideal positioning would be to focus on a niche and ensure you are not comparable, so that you actually do not need to compete by price or product.

Unfortunately, you do not need to start working on an idea if you **have no basic team** and can not market your product besides closing deals to **ensure the operations are financed** from start till fade out phase of the product.

In order to **gain your success** you need to do your part of the entreprenurial journey. Do not go the slow path. Go and **10X** your activities so that you achieve your goals. Make good use of your limited resources.

Act now!

For more information on Bletchley Park and how to visit the exhibition go to:

bletchleypark.org.uk/

HOW TO OVERCOME THE FEAR OF PUBLIC SPEAKING

By Katrin Israel (Estonia)

Experience removes fear

Often in our lives, there are so many skills that need polishing with time. The only way to do that is by repeating them again and again. One of these **skills** is public speaking. There are an abundant amount of people who have a fear of public speaking.

Often people suffer from sweats and they shiver when standing in front of a crowd. Moreover, people also often forget everything they prepared because **they go blank**.

All of this is because of the irrational fear in one's head that they might embarrass themselves or that they will not be able to do good enough.

Your fear is unnecessary

One thing which you need to do is acknowledge the fact that this fear you have is completely irrational.

This is the first thing you have to do in order to start overcoming it. Secondly, you need to face your fear as much as you can. The more you keep shying away from it, the more you will face difficulty with it. It will then keep on getting more and more intense.

The necessity is unavoidable

Remember that no matter what field you choose for yourself in your life, you will have to do public speaking. It is a skill that can take you places and really change the way people think about you or your business.

There are a lot of other exercises you can do in order to be more confident. You can start by speaking in front of the people with whom you are comfortable with and tell them to point out all the things that you need to improve.

What does your body language tell you

Another thing that you can do is speak in front of a mirror. Notice your **body language** and see **what you need to improve** so that you can better yourself more and more.

Nervosity is a good sign

Know that everybody is a little nervous before speaking in front of a crowd. You are not the only one struggling with it. Each time you have to speak in front of a lot of people, take a deep breath and refresh your mind.

Even if you forget something while you are presenting, you take some time to pause, breathe deeply and think about what you had to say and keep calm. This way what you forgot will come in your mind again and you will be good to go.

Body language is very important so don't keep a closed one. Whatever you decided to present, never cram it. Always make sure that you deliver it in a way **as if you are conversing with the crowd**.

If you cram the entire thing then you will panic each time you forget even a single word. If you speak your mind then you will face no such issues.

Avoid memorizing killing your confidence

You will also feel much more calm and confident **because the pressure of memorizing** will not be dangling on your head.

If you are one of the people who face this fear then the best thing you can do for yourself is jump at **every opportunity you get** where you have to speak in front of the crowd. The more you do it, the more you will realize that it is no big deal and can be easily done.

Be focused on stage

Now, the way you see the audience is also very important. Some people can make you more nervous than the other so you should **find one person you can focus on** but also keep looking around.

You don't necessarily have to look them in the eye, just look around and keep talking.

Bad advice that screws you up

The only "picturing the audience in their underwear" is **not a very effective way** because that is just going to shift your focus. Go with a clear mind and breathe so that you can stay relaxed for as long as you are there.

Speed is not everything - take time

Do not speak too fast because that way you will forget things and then end up panicking.

Never **go unprepared** because that will just make you **more nervous**. The best way to ease stress is by knowing your material. This will make you feel much more confident and comfortable.

Rehearse as **many times** as you can. This will ease you into the fact that you will not mess up when you are up there and you know what you are talking about.

Anyone can do it - overcome your fear

Many people out there think that public speaking is a skill that only a few people have but that is not true. Like any other skill, this can also be developed by anyone so there is nothing to worry about. ✐

 # OUR VISION

1 TO EMPOWER

2 20 MILLION PEOPLE

3 AROUND THE WORLD

4 TO GROW & EXPLODE THEIR BUSINESS

TOGETHER WE SUCCEED

BUSINESSBOOSTERTODAY.COM

BMW X7 - THE OFFROAD POWERHOUSE

By Christian Bartsch (Germany)

The BMW X7

The BMW X7 is the first car to fuse the **presence, exclusivity and spaciousness** of a luxury model with the agile and versatile driving properties expected of a **Sports Activity Vehicle** (SAV).

BMWs continued Growth

When I reflect upon the fact that over 20 years ago during my business training at the BMW HQ in Munich the first Z3 was introduced, the BMW Group has been growing its product pallete.

During my training I was part of the Rover project. Having to translate parts lists for the planed joint purchase project. It was an exiting time as the **diversity of the team** would show a young person how much power you can gain from a multinational team.

The X7 is a massive vehicle that has an impressive presence. It is so ahead of time in comparison to other competitor's products. The **advanced electronics and design** will positively surprise you.

Let me introduce to you this **powerhouse on 4 wheels**.

The BMW Vision iNext

The BMW Vision iNext marks the dawn of a new era in driving pleasure. This is the first time the strategic innovation fields of **Automated Driving, Connectivity, Electrification and Services** have been fully integrated in a single vehicle, which lends them **visual expression** with its future-focused design (D+ACES).

The areas of action the BMW Group has identified to ensure the company's sustained growth also include an **increased presence in the luxury segment**. The current offensive in this vehicle class is clearly evidenced by the new BMW X7.

Setting its sights on the future of driving pleasure: the BMW Vision iNext.

The BMW Vision iNEXT showcases the possibilities offered by **autonomous mobility** in the not too distant future. It demonstrates solutions designed first and foremost to inject fresh energy, all while focusing clearly on a **human-centric approach**. The production model based on the BMW Vision iNext will serve as the company's new technological flagship. According to BMW the first vehicles will be rolling off the assembly line at BMW Plant Dingolfing in **2021**.

Adopting the dimensions and proportions of a modern BMW Sports Activity Vehicle (SAV), the BMW Vision iNEXT presents an **authoritative figure**. Its pioneering character shines through in its clearly sculpted forms and surfaces. The car's front is dominated by the large BMW kidney grille. With no combustion engine to require cooling, the grille is blanked off and serves as an **"intelligence panel"** housing various sensors.

Slim headlights provide a modern take on BMW's signature **four-eyed front** silhouette. The BMW Vision iNEXT displays the powerful, **robust stance** of a modern BMW SAV when viewed from the side, while its functional two-box proportions and long

roofline hint at the generous space inside. Its long wheelbase and short overhangs, meanwhile, give the car's outline a dynamic powerhouse. Two large opposing doors and the **absence of B-pillars** ensure supreme ease of access to the car's interior, which takes the form of a snug and fashionably furnished "living space" on wheels.

New dimension in luxurious driving

The addition of the BMW X7 to the Bavarian premium carmaker's model portfolio opens up a **brand new dimension in luxurious driving** pleasure. The newest and also largest representative of the BMW X family blends **lavish presence, functionality and room-comfort** with the agile and supremely assured driving properties customers would expect from a Sports Activity Vehicle (SAV).

BMW's new design language brings the **modern elegance characteristic** of the brand's luxury-segment models to the exterior of the BMW X7, while also giving it a distinctly self-assured air.

Up to **three seat-rows or as a six-seater** with comfort seats offer remarkable levels of space, sophisticated design and *exclusive equipment*

features combine to give the cabin a truly luxurious feel.

Power under the bonnet

The line-up of engines for the brand's first luxury SAV comprises a **petrol V8** (not available in Europe), a six-cylinder in-line petrol unit and a pair of six-cylinder in-line diesels. All engines team up with an **eight-speed Steptronic transmission** and the BMW xDrive intelligent all-wheel-drive system. This ensures an unforgetable drivning experience.

Offroad & Executive Drive

The BMW X7 comes equipped as standard with **two-axle air suspension and Adaptive suspension** with electronically controlled dampers. Depending on the engine variant, customers also have the option of an M Sport differential and an Off-Road package, not to mention the **Executive Drive Pro** chassis system with active roll stabilisation.

The BMW X7 sticks to the formula of off-road ability combined with *impressive driving comfort and agile road handling* for

which its SAV models are renowned, courtesy of advanced powertrain and chassis technology.

The progressive luxury epitomised by the BMW X7 is further underlined by the broad spread of **cutting-edge driver assistance systems** on offer. The Driving Assistant Professional package (including the Steering and lane control assistant) and the Parking Assistant with Reversing Assistant most vividly embody the latest advances towards automated driving.

Also to be found on the list of standard equipment is the BMW Live Cockpit Professional, comprising a fully digital instrument cluster and Control Display each with a screen diagonal of 12.3 inches.

Plus, the new BMW Operating System 7.0 enables optimised **multimodal operation** using the iDrive Controller, the **touchscreen display**, the steering wheel buttons, or voice and **gesture control**.

Inside Experience

The new BMW X7 isn't shy. Charismatic design features make it stand out, from the new one-piece kidney grille to the expressive lines that flow elegantly to the **eye-catching**

3D L-shaped LED taillights. Add to this the brilliant 21" light alloy wheels, and curious eyes won't know where to look.

Sitting in the new BMW X7 simply feels different. It still evokes that unique BMW feeling with its Individual Extended Merino leather upholstery and **dynamic ambient lighting**; however, thanks to the Panorama Glass Sunroof, which comes as standard, and the new optional 6-seat configuration with two captain-style comfort seats in the second row, it also has the power to surprise the senses.

Enjoy a Massage

The standard Comfort seats for driver and front passenger in the BMW X7 immerse you in an overwhelming feeling of relaxation and comfort. The Massage function, available as optional equipment, for the driver and front passenger helps to improve the physical well-being by stimulating or relaxing certain muscle groups. There are eight massage programmes dedicated to different parts of the body. There are three intensity levels. Exclusively available as part of the Premium package.

Wheel Design

At 22 inches, the optional light alloy Multi-spoke style 757 wheels, exclusively available for xDrive4i and xDrive3d models, are among the **largest wheels** in the portfolio and thus radiate an unmistakable presence when viewed from the side. Finished in Bicolour, they look particularly noble.

Overall Conclusion

The vehicle body looks **more powerful, refined and luscious** with the lavish surfaces without losing the sportiness that is typical to BMW.

Especially in their large and particularly luxurious vehicles, BMW attaches great importance to a marked appearance and the maximum possible **feel-good factor** in the interior. It's about freedom – and the feeling of being at home in a BMW.

The design has to arouse strong emotions while expressing the highest quality and durability at the same time. In order to be able to spend **every moment intensely, full of meaning and beauty**. The X7 designer team have achieved to succeed at this massive challenge they set for the design of this new BMW. ✈

BUSINESS LESSONS FROM SCUBA DIVING

By Marina Kotze (South Africa)

A nearly life-long dream fairly recently finally realized when I was able to participate in and complete my PADI Open Water Scuba Diving qualification in the pristine marine protected reserve of Sodwana Bay, South Africa. You can imagine my excitement when the opportunity presented itself and I found myself in class learning everything I needed to know to dive with the appropriate gear to a maximum depth of 18 meters below the deep sea's surface. I was thrilled at the thought that my goal of finally learning how to scuba dive, will soon be achieved.

During my training over the course of five days, I could not help but notice the **similarities between the sport of scuba diving and doing business**. My mind was flooded with light bulb after light bulb that went on with sound business principles that I was able to apply during my diving training. Following below are some **key business lessons** applicable to scuba diving and vice versa:

Embarking on a new project requires a true, innate desire to accomplish your goal: I was able to successfully complete my scuba diving qualification because I absolutely *wanted* to. That is actually one of the "rules" when applying for you PADI Open Water Scuba Diving qualification – one should be internally motivated to do it, and not because you are feeling pressured by relatives or friends. This example applies for any business endeavour – you are driven and motivated by a deep-seated WHY, the fire that keeps you going, even when you don't feel like doing what needs to be done. Being internally motivated will help you to stay disciplined in achieving your goals and reaching your business destination.

To achieve something new and different requires your full attention: We know that broken focus is a very real reason why people fail at any given task. During my scuba diving training, I had to make sure that I am fully *present* and completely in the *here and now* throughout every aspect of the program. Scuba diving is a potentially life-threatening sport, and not being fully focused and missing out on crucial information could have very serious consequences later. I felt like my life depended on gaining and retaining this essential information. The same applies during business endeavours – being laser focused increases productivity and greatly helps to not miss out on important information and detail, which are always important factors in securing business deals.

To achieve something you have never done before requires input from a qualified outside source: To me, this stood out head and shoulders above all else during my scuba diving training – the fact that I am taught by the best qualified and experienced instructors. They understood where I was coming from, what it takes to work and learn through the course material, and, as a result, they were able to successfully and skilfully guide me with patience and professionalism. I am forever grateful towards my instructors for playing a major role in making my dream come true! Who are you looking towards for guidance and input in any or even all of your business endeavours? No one can succeed alone in life or business, because there is always someone more qualified than you to show and teach you the things you do not know yet… Always be open and humble to learn from the best, and never shy away from asking for help.

Your ability to follow very specific instructions could mean the difference between success and failure: In order to qualify as a scuba diver, I had to perform in and complete a variety of tests during several different dives. The requirements are specific to the T and based on one's ability to exactly and precisely follow instructions. In business, it implies that instruction from coaches and leaders in the field should be followed in the same fashion. A "know it all" attitude or mindset will highly likely result in failure, as specific instructions were not adhered to.

Great journeys and projects are best accomplished with a "buddy" on your side: Another "rule" in scuba diving is to never dive alone; to always dive with a dive buddy and a dive master. The simple reason is for safety purposes. Your buddy and you have each other's backs, looking out for potential dangers, and provide any necessary support during a dive. The dive master makes sure that everyone has a fun and safe dive.

Your journey as an entrepreneur and business owner should also be one where you are surrounded by all the necessary support from loved ones and team members. Each supportive person in your life should play a constructive role in your life and to such an extent that you know you could not have achieved success if not for your support structure.

Preparation is key and vital to your success: For you experienced scuba divers, you know the drill prior to embarking on an exciting dive! There's a very specific checklist of things to prepare and do before hitting the ocean surface. Again, all to ensure a safe and enjoyable dive! How and in what way are you preparing, for example, for business meetings? How do you prepare to close a deal? And how do you prepare yourself to achieve your specific business goals? And remember, planning is a vital step as part of any preparation.

> "Planning and preparation go hand in hand to ensure a highly likely positive outcome in any given situation." – Marina Kotzé

Stay calm during the storm: Things might not always go as planned and prepared; therefore, one should also plan and prepare for the *unplanned* and *unprepared*. Conditions and circumstances can change at any given time, and there are no guarantees for anything in life and in business. In such situations, the only thing we do have control over is our own reaction. When the unexpected happens – and rest assured that it always does – it is of vital importance to always stay calm and not to panic. Once again, scuba divers know the drill. Why? Because of our training. During my very first dive in the deep Indian Ocean, there was a storm at sea and a strong surge and underwater current. After completing all my tests on the ocean floor and coming up to surface, I became extremely nauseous due to being swayed back and forth by the surge. And on top of that, when I finally surfaced, waves were crushing over my head and, in the process, the buoy came down hitting me through the face and slamming my mask off. The key for me was to stay calm, not to panic and then think about what to do AND then to perform another test at the surface where my instructor was waiting for me. Fortunately, all went well, and man was I grateful to be back safely in the boat!

A positive attitude makes everything better: During my diving experience in a pretty rough sea, it was crucial for me to maintain a positive mental attitude. I viewed the whole experience during the rain, wind and waves as an exciting adventure of a lifetime! And, as a result, my unique first diving experience was all the more memorable. As with deep sea diving, life and business, a positive frame of mind is often the key to help us through challenging times. A positive frame of mind helps one to view difficulties as temporary, which will make success and victory taste even sweeter.

> "Remember, hard times are there to test us, so stay calm, be positive and know that tough people outlast tough situations!" – Marina Kotzé ✦

RESIDENTIAL REAL ESTATE INVESTMENT IN THE USA

By Paul Kazanofski (USA)

Being an entrepreneur and being successful is never easy. I have been an entrepreneur all my life. I never went to college, and never had a job working for anyone else.

For people who want to get into real estate, DON'T BELIEVE what you see on TV. It is a very rewarding business but it is also a difficult business that requires patience and longevity to be successful in the field.

Mentorship

For me, my success in real estate has come from great coaching, mentorship, and a lot of blood, sweat and tears. This helped me become the investor that I am today and achieving success in the industry. In order to ensure your safety in the investing world, there 2 areas that are most important.

First, it is imperative to have mentors & coaches especially when you first get into the business. This is 100% not a get rich quick scheme business. Having the **right skills, knowledge & patience** is the best way to build your net worth & portfolio by buying, holding and fixing up property using other people's money. You can also then get bank money to do cash out refinancing and keep long term rentals to enjoy positive cash flow.

You must also **have strong discipline** for this strategy of building wealth to be successful. In the last 10 years, my company and I have flipped over 350 houses. With the profits I bought rentals the same way & kept several dozens of them for positive cash flow. Some real estate investors who don't want to handle the management of a property contract with a property management company for a fixed or percentage fee.

This takes some weight off an investor's shoulders, transforming the real estate into a more passive investment. However, this trade off also means that an investor cedes some control of their properties and lose a portion of their monthly income.

Critical Mistakes

Real estate is different animal in that you must know your numbers before you go into any transaction. The market in the US is **very attractive** right now, so there are a lot of people getting into the industry and **making critical mistakes**. Some of these mistakes are buying in the wrong location, buying a house that is very distressed and requiring a solid knowledge base in construction, or worse yet in a bad neighbourhood, also referred to as a war zone.

The most important thing is to buy the property right. The fact is the **profit is made on the purchase** and not just on the sale. There are plenty of people that make this mistake over and over again. The way we get our deals is by us doing door knocking and meeting with motivated sellers who are under some kind of distress situation such as foreclosure or a short sale. We also do direct mail to folks with low to high equity.

Consider these elements

When purchasing single family homes, town homes, duplexes or small multi-family units / properties, here are a few things you should consider:

A lot of people want to get in the real estate game but, you can not play the game if you don't know the rules.

It is well documented that most millionaires are made from real estate investing. Real Estate is the best way to create wealth in the USA or anywhere in the world.

A lot of people read a book or watch a TV show and think they are ready for real estate investing. However, that is not the case. I have seen many people lose money without the appropriate training, knowledge and coaching.

House-flipping is the most active, hands-on way to invest in real estate. In a house flip, an investor purchases a home, makes changes and renovations to improve it's value on the market, and then sells it a higher price. House-flipping is generally short-term, because the longer the investor owns the home without leasing it to tenants, the more their expenses add up. This eats away at their profits because most of the time you are borrowing other people's money at a higher interest rate. Called OPM or Other People's Money, investors use OPM to make renovations to the home to increase its value or sell when its value in the housing market increases.

Purchase Price

Remember this - just because it is a distressed property in foreclosure does not necessarily mean it is a good deal. Banks do not always price them right or try to get the most possible amount for their asset. This is where the investor has to be very knowledgeable on how to buy the property right. Primarily, you must know your numbers.

Typically, you must buy these properties for 65% of the After Repair Value (AVR) minus the repair budget which then gives you the maximum allowable offer. Remember to stick by these numbers to ensure you stay safe in the deal. It doesn't matter what you are buying, whether it is a commercial property or single-family home. A great investor says no countless times before he says yes to a

property. We typically do 80 offers before we find a diamond in the rough. If you do not follow the system in which to buy the property correctly, it is the beginning of the end of your real estate investing endeavour. Typically, most people lose money because of lack of knowledge in construction, and don't understand how to design and fix up the property correctly.

You must also build the proper relationships with contractors & subcontractors so you will not be ripped off. It is important to know who you are dealing with and check out their credentials before you work with them.

If you watch HGTV, then you have probably watched a house get transformed from rags to riches in under 30 minutes and sold for a sizeable profit by house-flipping pros. In these shows, house-flippers buy a home that they believe to be underpriced, add value through renovations — such as replacing countertops or flooring, or tearing down walls to change floor plans — and then selling the home at a higher price to turn a profit.

While **house-flipping** is exciting, it also requires deep financial and real estate knowledge to ensure that you can make over the home within time and budget constraints to ensure a profit in the housing market when the home is sold. The success — and the financial burden — of a house flip falls entirely on the investor.

You need enough cash for a down payment and/or good enough credit to secure a home loan in order to buy a property before another flipper does. It's a high-pressure and high-stakes real estate investment that makes for great TV, but a good investment opportunity only for certain knowledgeable investors.

Risky Wholesaling Activities

Another property-flipping option is called wholesaling. Wholesaling is when an investor signs a contract to buy a property that they believe is underpriced and then sells it quickly to another investor at a higher price for a profit. Most often, wholesalers seek out properties in need of renovations and sell them to house-flippers who are willing to perform the renovations.

An investor will sign a contract to buy a property and put down an earnest-money deposit. Then, they quickly try to sell the home to a house-flipper at a premium, earning a small profit. Essentially, a wholesaler gets a finder's fee for brokering a home sale to a house-flipper.

However, unlike traditional brokers, a wholesaler uses their position as the homebuyer to broker the deal. By working with wholesalers, we can cast a wider net with these relationships to find more deals to work. It is important in business to create and build these relationships with people in the industry, when you show them you are a real cash buyer, it pays back real dividends. People come to you first when they have a deal. After all, it is not just what you know, it is who knows you. If you are not branded correctly, you will not position yourself to be pre-eminent in your market.

Wholesaling is a risky venture, also requiring real estate and financial expertise. It demands due diligence and access to a network of house-flippers in order to find a buyer within a time frame to sell at a profitable price. Otherwise, like house-flipping, you risk not earning a profit or, worse, losing money.

Rental properties also require hands-on management, but unlike house flips, they have a long-term investment horizon. Any type of property (residential, commercial, or industrial) can be a rental property. Property owners earn regular cash flow usually on a monthly basis in the form of rental payment from tenants. This can provide a steady, reliable income stream for investors, but it also requires a lot of work or delegation of responsibilities to ensure that operations are running smoothly.

First, you must find tenants for your property. This may be easy or difficult depending on your property type and available resources for finding tenants. You are also responsible for performing background screenings for prospective tenants (if you want to) and providing legally sound lease agreement contracts with tenants. For each month that you do not have a tenant, you miss out on income from your investment.

Once you have tenants, you have a litany of resultant duties. As the landlord, you are responsible for rent collection, property maintenance, repairs, evictions, record-keeping for the properties and ensuring legal compliance on all matters.

This can be your passion

Depending on the number of rental properties that you own, property management can be a part-time or full-time job. Remember, enter at your own risk. I knew I would be an entrepreneur since I was 13 years old, scalping tickets and buying products for cheaper, and selling for a profit. It takes this kind of drive and hustle to make it in any business, especially the real estate business. ✐

PROPERTY SOURCING PROFITS:

YOUR 5-STEP GUIDE

By John Stokoe (United Kingdom)

STEP TWO - FIND YOUR DEAL

How do I find investor-grade opportunities?

Once you've identified your target area, you can turn your attention to finding, negotiating and securing property deals. There are a number of different ways to identify and acquire property but let's start with the most obvious – Estate Agents.

Estate Agents

Estate Agents are the most relied upon means of finding and acquiring new property and if managed well, can be a valuable source of new opportunities for your sourcing business. However, all too often we see investors and sourcing agents alike making offers at 20-30% below market value with no explanation. *Remember,* estate agents are there to sell houses and make a commission, so if you're consistently offering 20-30% below market value with no explanation, it's unlikely you're going to work together very long.

Instead, we suggest being honest and transparent with agents from the get-go. When you walk into an estate agent's office for the first time, introduce yourself and tell them what you do. Be personable, **outline the value you can bring** to their business if they're open to the idea of working together, and share your professional accreditations with them. Explain the way in which you calculate your offers and **help them understand** the **type of deals** you are looking for. Operating in this way will immediately set you apart from the amateurs out there and help them to see that you, like them, are simply an agent who broker deals **on behalf of investors and clients.**

By communicating openly and **collaborating with estate agents** you can quickly build up good rapport and in time they will come to see the value you can provide to their business—**helping them shift seemingly 'unsellable' houses**. Also, consider listing any acquired properties houses back with the selling estate agent and in time you can develop a powerful network of referring agents who will put you on speed dial for properties their struggling to sell. Over the past three years we've built some excellent relationships with estate agents and we now have agents bringing deals directly to us so it's well worth taking that time to build those relationships.

HOWEVER, it's also worth noting that estate agents should only represent one arm of your sourcing business. Many of the best property deals never even make it to the open market!

To find the best opportunities, you need to get creative—and that means using alternative strategies to get great property deals to coming to **you**…

Alternative Strategies

Person to person

- **Word-of-mouth** Start with what you already have. Ask you friends, family, current and previous clients for a few names of people who are having trouble selling their houses. The more people the better. You don't ask, you don't get!
- **For Sale boards**. Take the time to knock on doors and introduce yourself. If a vendor is looking to sell their property and you can help, they'll likely listen. This is a great way to get direct-to-vendor and understand their current situation.
- **Networking events**. Go to property and business networking events. Introduce yourself, build relationships and tell people about what you do—who knows you may stumble onto a struggling landlord looking for a way out!
- **Local labourers and contractors**. Take the time to speak with local tradesmen/women. They naturally network with a range of local landlords, vendors and agents, so they will often know of individuals looking to sell and be able to refer you on.

Online Media

- **Social media**. Join Facebook Buy/Sell groups in your sourcing area and actively promote what you're doing on social media. It's truly amazing the opportunities that can arise from simply telling people what you are doing.
- **Websites**. Setting up multiple websites to help people sell their home is a great way to acquire new leads. Be sure to include relevant keywords to improve your search rankings and offer people a clear value proposition; for example, an offer on any property in 48hrs.
- **Online adverts**. Classified newspaper ads may be on the decline but online advertising is booming. Independent buy/sell sites like Gumtree and Craigslist can be a valuable source of new leads if you take the time to create effective ads.

Offline Media

- **Local newspaper** Primarily used by the older community looking to downsize or sell, classified ads in local newspapers can still bring in high-quality leads. Again, invest time in understanding which publications and ads are most effective.
- **Direct Mail.** Identify empty houses in your area. Acquire the owner details from land registry and create a direct-to-vendor letter campaign to identify motivated sellers in your area.
- **Flyers**. Flyers are still very effective! Create your ads and be systematic in your distribution. Persistence and regular distribution is key to making this strategy a success.

Calculating your offer

Running the numbers and calculating your maximum offer is a straightforward process, but does require a little more explanation. For a step-by-step on how to calculate your offer, be sure to attend our free webinar where we'll walk you through several example deals! ↗